101 Fun Things To Do With A GoPro® Camera

Jim R. Larsen

DEDICATION

Dedicated to my dear wife, who tolerates me well during these expeditions to take strange pictures. And she lets me spend countless hours at the computer writing my many manuscripts.

CONTENTS

ACKNOWLEDGMENTS

GoPro® is a registered trademark of GoPro Inc. This book is not authorized or endorsed by GoPro Inc.

All trade names mentioned in this text are the property of their respective owners.

Thank you to my friend Sean for the proof reading and editing help.

Special thanks to Nick Woodman for inventing the GoPro® camera. You are a HERO.

Warning!

Participating in extreme sports activities may result in injury or death. Know your limits and always choose activities that you are able to perform safely. Do not attempt risky maneuvers without proper training and supervision. The reader assumes all responsibility for the risks associated with activities undertaken after reading this book.

The Ground Rules

Respect People's Privacy

Hidden camera photography was not considered an option for any of the ideas collected for this book (well, maybe one). People are concerned about privacy these days, and do not want to be photographed without their consent, especially in ways that entertain others at their expense. Make sure that people are aware they are being photographed if they are in a location where privacy is an assumption.

Obey the Law

New laws are being written every year to restrict aerial drone photography. If you use your camera on a radio controlled craft, check with local ordinances to be sure you are in compliance. At the time of this writing there are many restrictions on the commercial use of drones for photography, but there are very few laws restricting the non-professional use.

Don't Get Hurt

Always observe your surroundings to make sure you are safe when using your GoPro® camera. Be aware of power lines, holes in the ground, swift river currents, cliffs, and any other risks you may encounter when making you ultimate movie. Plan for safety as you plan all your shots.

Jim R. Larsen

101 Fun Things to Do with a GoPro® Camera

Anchor Inspection

You have anchored your boat in a quiet cove for an overnight stay. Is your anchor secure? Find out with your GoPro®. Use the waterproof housing. Secure the camera to a weighted line. Row out to a position in front of the boat and lower the camera until it is near the bottom. With the camera a few feet off the bottom, row slowly in the direction of the anchor line until you have passed over the point where the anchor is sitting on the bottom. Pull your camera up and review the footage to see if your anchor is set securely.

Aquarium Cam

Any camera can take pictures from the outside of an aquarium. With the GoPro® camera and the waterproof housing you can get right in the middle of the action in your aquarium. Set the camera up to peer into favorite fish hiding spots, or to catch the feeding frenzy.

Archery

Use a clamping camera mount to position the camera on your bow to catch the action from several angles. The Jaws Clamp Mount will let the camera stand off the bow and create a good angle to capture the shot. You can even create some camera angles to capture the shooter in the frame as well as the bow and arrow. Another camera near the target, looking back at the shooter, will give you some pictures that you would never dare to take while holding the camera.

Athletic Training

Athletic trainers are increasingly using video feedback to help review proper technique when teaching skills specific to a sport. The GoPro®

camera is perfect for this. Its small size and high resolution images make it possible to get great images from many angles. Use video playback or stop action time-lapse photography to analyze a golf swing, a karate kick, a tennis serve, or any athletic skill you are working on.

Attic Inspection

Have you ever wanted to look into your attic, but for some reason you did not want to (or just couldn't) crawl up there to see what's going on? Send in your GoPro® camera! Mount the camera on a broom handle, monopod, or a pole. Open the attic access hatch and shine as much light in there as you can. Start the camera rolling and raise it up into the attic. You can monitor the results in real time on your smartphone or tablet using the Wi-Fi feature found on many GoPro® cameras, or you can record the video and watch it on your computer after you are done taking a few panoramas of your mysterious hidden spaces.

Awesome Selfies

Selfies on a cell phone are so, well, ordinary! The monopod camera mount is an awesome tool for "selfie" photography. The monopod is a telescoping pole that can be as short as one foot long, or extendable to be several feet long. You get to point the camera at yourself to record outrageous action video or stills while you perform your best stunts and activities. Many people use a monopod to capture themselves as they are hiking or riding.

Baseball Fielding

Think for a moment of all the fun camera angles you can create with a GoPro® camera during a baseball game. Fielders can wear the camera on their body or their head, or on a monopod that elevates the camera behind them. Capture all the action on the infield as players are tagged, flies are caught, and runs are scored.

Basketball

Mount your GoPro® camera behind the glass backboard before your next basketball game. Edit the footage from the hoop in with additional footage of the game for a great sports video.

Bicycle (Road Bike)

The GoPro® camera is capable of many creative camera angles on a bicycle. The camera can be used in several ways: facing forward to show the rider's point of view, facing backwards to capture the action behind them, or a combination of both that also includes a view of the pedals, gears, chain, or brakes. Bicycle riding, when not in the woods, is a good application for the monopod that elevates the camera above the rider. It can be attached to a mast mounted on the bike, or on an extension from the rider's body or helmet. Use care whenever you make an attachment to a helmet or person that you do not create a risk for injury should the camera strike an object or get hung up on something.

Bird Nest Watching

Mount your GoPro® camera next to a bird's nest in a tree and start capturing some great close up nature pictures right in your back yard. Experiment with video, stills, or time-lapse modes for some interesting results. Use the Wi-Fi feature to see the action in real time, or collect your camera after a while and view the results on your computer.

Boat Hull Inspection

Use the waterproof housing for this one. Clamp the camera to your boat hook and start the video. Guide the camera and the boat hook around your boat to capture a video (or still shots) of the underwater surface of your hull. Find out what is wrapped around your propeller, view the condition of the rudder, or look to see if that recent bump you felt has caused any serious damage.

Bow Cam (Hunting)

If you used your GoPro® camera to get good shots of your archery practice, why not use it on the hunt? Mount your camera on your bow in a manner that does not interfere with the balance or the action of the bow. Silence the beeps and turn off the LED status light so that it does not spook your game. Now just press the button to start recording as you take aim at your trophy.

Children at Play

We have all seen the home videos of children playing. Jazz them up a bit by splicing in some video from the child's perspective, or from the perspective of one of their toys. Think about how you might use a chest mounted camera to capture a new perspective on baby's first steps.

Cooking

There are many creative ways one can use a GoPro® camera to capture all the action in the kitchen while cooking a meal. Cameras mounted over work areas or over the stove can capture the action while you prepare or cook food. You can also use the time-lapse feature to get an interesting perspective on how the whole meal came together.

Crab Pot Cam

Here is another good use of your waterproof housing. Mount the camera inside or outside of your crab pot. Set the pot in water that does not exceed the rated depth for your waterproof housing (which is just under 200 feet). If you attach the camera to the line so that it is looking down from several feet over the pot you might also see a few of the big ones that got away.

Dash Cam

Have you ever seen someone driving so badly that you wished you had caught it on video? A dash cam is a video camera that is usually set to record the events that are seen while looking forward through the windshield. The GoPro® camera with a clamp mount can be attached to the dash of your car so that it captures all the traffic action that you are seeing as you drive. Much of the footage is likely to be something you just delete at the end of the day. But then on that one day when you are behind that crazy driver who is cutting everyone off, you might just be recording the next great YouTube® viral hit.

Diving into Water with a Monopod

This is a popular variation of the action selfie. This will require the waterproof housing. Use a monopod to hold the camera so it is looking back at you, and keep it rolling as you jump into the pool doing your best belly flop ever. If you are lucky, the camera will keep looking at you in the underwater portion of your dive too.

Drums

Mount one or more GoPro® cameras on the drum set to capture some interesting action shots for a music video. Drum sets offer lots of options for clamping a camera onto a cymbal stand or other hardware attachment point. Or suspend the camera on a microphone boom directly overhead for an interesting top-down view.

Extreme Ironing

Yes, there really is a sport called Extreme Ironing. Look it up! People take an iron and an ironing board into an extreme sporting environment and are photographed while pressing some clothes. The GoPro® camera can take this sport to new levels with live action shots that were never possible before. This may be a great time to add a helmet cam or a body camera to the video mix.

Film the Tide Coming in

Have you ever wondered how life on the beach changes when the water comes in and covers everything up? Secure your GoPro® camera in a waterproof housing and secure it to a heavy object on the beach at low tide. The tide will be low again in about 13 hours, so you need to plan appropriately. You may be able to go swimming to retrieve your camera, or you may want to wait. Plan your photo shoot so that the sun will be high when the camera is under water. This will provide the best possible light. Time-lapse photography will provide longer battery life than full motion video. Your completed project will show the water coming in to cover the beach and the camera, and it will hopefully reveal the sea life that comes into the frame after the water arrives.

Find a Rattle Under Your Car

Do you wish you knew what was making that strange sound under the back of your car when you drive over a speed bump? Maybe your GoPro® camera can help. Secure the camera under the car so that it has a view of the suspect area. Drive just far enough to make the sound happen, then check the video to see if it shows the offending mechanism. Do this in a place away from traffic, such as on private property or in an empty parking lot. That will help avoid accidents, and it will also make it easy to recover your camera in case it falls off!

Fishing (Underwater View)

The GoPro® camera with its waterproof housing can add some interesting fun to your next fishing trip. Attach the camera to a pole or to a monopod and dangle your bait within view of the camera. Capture some live action footage of the big catch of the day. Or use the camera to probe into that deep hole in the creek to see how many big fish are lurking in there. If you are crafty you can create a camera mount that will attach to your fishing line near the sinker, pointed at your bait or lure.

Get Close to Dangerous Wildlife

Getting a close up video of a venomous snake or an alligator used to mean getting close to the danger, but now you can use your GoPro® camera and stay out of harm's way. You can use a passive approach by setting the camera up at a place where the animals will likely pass by, or you can take a more active approach and attach the camera to a long pole and use that to approach the scene.

Grocery Cart

Grocery shopping just became a whole lot more interesting. Attach your GoPro® camera to the cart to use video or time-lapse photography to capture the shopping experience. Speed up the video during playback for a fun view of an old activity. This could be even more interesting if someone was riding in the cart.

Guitar Playing

Attach a GoPro® camera to a guitar to capture some interesting angles during a performance for a music video. The Jaws Clamp Mount can attach to the head of the guitar to view the fingerboard, or to the body of the guitar to view the picking hand. Some thoughtful direction will even get a good view of the rest of the band from this interesting onboard perspective.

Gun Cam

Hunters may enjoy mounting a GoPro® camera so that it sights down the side of their rifle during a hunting trip. The LED lights can be turned off or covered, and the beeps can be disabled so that the camera does not interfere with the hunt. Keeping the video rolling will also provide you with a good safety review. Later you can check the video to make sure you never pointed the weapon at anything you shouldn't have.

Gutter Inspection

How can you inspect the gutters on a two story house to see if they need cleaning? You may not be interested in climbing that high up a ladder. Attach the GoPro® camera to a long pole and send it up on the roof to inspect your gutters for you. Use the Wi-Fi feature to view the video on your tablet or smartphone in real time, or view the video on your computer after the shooting is completed.

Hang Gliding

The GoPro® camera has had a noticeable impact on the videos we see from hang gliders. The small size and weight of the camera make it possible to mount the camera in ways that capture both the pilot and the scenery in the same frame. And you may not have to actually be on the hang glider to get that shot. Take your camera out to the flight area and you can probably talk a pilot into letting you mount your camera on their craft. Let the pilot tell you where and how to mount the camera so that it will remain secure and not interfere with the flight controls.

Hang It from Lines

How about getting some great action shots while hovering over some whitewater rapids in the middle of a river? If you can throw a line across the river, you can use it to suspend your GoPro® camera in the middle of the action. This may be a good time to add a little brightly colored floatation to the back of your waterproof enclosure, just in case the camera falls in the river. If two people are positioned to hold each end of the line they can manipulate the camera position for the best dramatic shot.

Helium Balloons

Here is a very inexpensive way to send your GoPro® camera high into the air. Suspend the camera below a dozen or more helium filled party balloons. Attach a line from your fishing pole as a tether so that it doesn't get away from you. You may also be able to attach a tail fin to the camera so that it always points in the same direction relative to the breeze, making it easier to point the camera in the desired direction. After the shot just reel in the line to bring the camera back down to earth.

Hide It in a Dog Toy and Play Fetch

This requires the right dog and the right toy. The toy needs to be tough enough to protect the camera, and the dog needs to be gentle enough to prevent damage. Some retriever breeds are known for their soft mouth. With careful planning and preparation you will be able to create a camera housing that will let you capture the flight of the dog toy through the air and then the trip back with the dog.

Hide It on Stage at Your Wedding

This is an acceptable exception to our "no hidden camera" rule, because you are photographing yourself, or you are photographing a wedding party that knows you are taking their picture. The small size of the GoPro® camera makes it possible to hide it in the flowers or in a candelabrum on stage for an up-close view of the faces of the bride and groom. If hiding the camera is not a concern, consider having the wedding officiant wear the camera with a chest strap for the best stage view of all.

Hot Air Balloon

There are more places to mount a camera on a hot air balloon than one might imagine. There are easy mounting opportunities on the framework of the gondola. An interesting perspective is possible by mounting the camera on a line hanging off a high point on the balloon envelope so that it points at the passengers. Some balloon captains have also mounted cameras inside the balloon to look down and provide a unique view that very few people get to see.

Hula Hoop

Carefully mount your GoPro® camera on the outside of a hula hoop. Point the camera in for a fun gyrating view of the hula-hooper. Point the camera outward for a unique gyrating panoramic viewpoint.

Jet Ski

Jet skis can be hooked up with cameras using methods similar to filming onboard motorcycles and bicycles. A mast mounted camera behind the driver provides a fun point of view that includes the driver along with a great view of all the exciting action. When there are multiple jet skis with cameras involved, teach the drivers where to position themselves relative to one another during their best stunts and tricks. Use a mounting angle that shoots to the side or to the back of the Jet Ski for this. You don't want Jet Skis attempting to do stunts directly in front of another moving vehicle.

Jetpack

Water powered jet packs are here! These awesome toys use streams of water to lift a pilot up to 40 feet above the surface of a lake or bay. This is a perfect application for a GoPro® camera in a waterproof enclosure. Edit your video to include additional shots from the perspective of an onlooker. The jet pack can even propel the pilot underwater, so be sure the mountings are secure and that safety tethers are attached to the cameras.

Kayaking

There are many kinds of kayaking, including fishing trips, gentle trips across a pond or lake, expedition kayaking in large bodies of water, and whitewater river running. You will need choose a camera angle based on the perspective you want to capture and the type of kayaking being done. The camera can be attached directly to the boat hull and pointed at the paddler or at the water. A rear facing camera on the back of a whitewater kayak will capture the action of the boat behind the camera boat. Another option is to build a short mast to elevate the camera two or three feet above the boat. This lets you get some good shots of the paddler without using an angle that films up their nose!

Keyboard

Position a GoPro® camera on a stand and point it at the keyboard player's hands for some interesting views of the keyboardist playing for a music video. Careful camera placement can also provide you with a view of the other band members in the frame of the shot. Unlike the guitar mounted camera, this one will not be moving around and the shots can be set up very carefully and thoughtfully.

Kite Surfing

Kite surfing is a popular extreme sport that can send riders high into the air for jumps and flips. You will definitely want a waterproof enclosure for this shot. Use (or build) a lightweight mount that can clamp onto one of the kite lines several feet above the rider, or consider attaching it near the kite itself. A kite mounted camera can also be used as a controllable camera platform for capturing footage of other riders doing stunts within range of the camera.

Lecture/Training Recorder

One of the popular early uses for cassette recorders was to record college lectures, and then play them back to help study for a test. Cell phones are sometimes used for that task now. Using a GoPro® camera to record the lecture allows you to also capture all the PowerPoint slides and whiteboard illustrations too.

Look Behind the Couch

Use your GoPro® camera to look under or behind heavy furniture that you can't move. Mount the camera on a monopod or a pole and set it to record, then use the pole to send the camera into those spaces you need to explore. You may even be able to send the camera inside the sofa to see if there is enough loose change in there to pay for a pizza or something.

Look Behind the Refrigerator

Children, dogs, and cats have one thing in common. They all have small toys that can roll into that tiny space around a refrigerator. You can discover these little treasures every 10 years or so when you move your refrigerator out and clean behind it. Or you can check under your refrigerator now by putting your GoPro® camera on a monopod and then reaching down behind the refrigerator with the camera and filming the bottom from the back side. You can use the Wi-Fi feature to view the video feed in real time.

Look Down a Well

Treasure hunters have been known to find valuable artifacts in the bottom of old wells. You can use a GoPro® camera in a waterproof enclosure to explore the well bottom first, before risking a trip down into the well yourself. Attach the camera to a weighted line and lower it on to the bottom of the well, then view the video to see what treasures await you. If the well is dark, you can brighten things up a little by adding a waterproof LED flashlight to the camera mount before sending it down to the dark depths.

Look Under the Bed

Why not? We have already looked under the couch and behind the refrigerator. Many of us are known to have a hoard of treasures hidden under the bedframe. Get a quick inventory of what's in there before you start dragging it all out by sending in the GoPro® on a monopod.

Luggage Security Cam

Have you ever wondered where you luggage goes when you check it in at the airport? Drill a hole through the shell of your suitcase and mount your GoPro® camera inside, looking out. With a little luck you will get to see the long journey taken by your bags. And if you want to know if anyone is looking in your bag for inspection, set up a camera to that it captures footage of anyone who opens the lid of your suitcase. If you are one of the unlucky ones who has things stolen from your bag, the camera will catch them (unless they steal your GoPro®).

Magnifier

Sometimes the job requires you to read fine print on a label that is impossible to see. It might be because of poor lighting, the position of the label, or those silly bifocals that aren't ever in the right place when you need them. The high definition pictures taken with a GoPro® camera can be zoomed up many times, making fine print as easy to read as a movie poster.

Make an Orbiting 360 Degree Pole Mount

It is an interesting special effect in the movies when the camera suddenly takes a circle around the star and shows them from all sides in a quick panoramic orbit. You can accomplish the effect by building an orbiting boom. Mount the boom on a pole with the camera facing in to the center, and mount the boom on top of a pole. Hold the pole and spin the camera around you for an orbiting panorama. Careful design of the boom can keep most of it out of sight of the camera. Now think of ways you can apply this technology to other scenes, such as mounting it to the roof of a car to rotate around and capture an orbiting panorama of the outside of the car. Or hang your pole mount on a ceiling fan and give it a push to let it slowly coast around the room (don't turn it on, it will go too fast!)

Miniature Golf

Miniature golf just cries out with creative photographic opportunities! Small cameras can be placed on or near the greens, inside obstacles, on putters, or at the bottom of a hole. A stable camera standing off at a distance can capture the whole round of golf with time-lapse photography. Edit the many views together for a fun memory of your day at the miniature golf course.

Moto Cross

Moto Cross dirt bike riding is exciting and dangerous. Capture the action up close and personal with GoPro® cameras on the rider's helmet, on the rider's body, and at various interesting angles on the bike itself. Edit these shots in with spectator perspectives for an interesting and thrilling video about this exciting sport.

Motorcycle Road Trip

The GoPro® camera can be used to capture great footage on road bikes too. People who ride sport bikes together as a group should consider camera mounting positions that not only show the bike and rider, but also capture some of the others in the group in the frame at the same time. Mounting cameras on several bikes in a group will give you great material to edit together with some driving music. The cameras should be mounted in a manner that requires no attention from the rider. Start recording before you hit the road and let it run until the battery runs out.

Mount It on an Egg Timer and Take a 360 Degree Time-lapse Panorama

An egg timer is a mechanical timer that you wind up and it runs for the prescribed amount of time and then dings at the end. Mounting the camera to the dial of the egg timer will give you a camera stand that rotates one revolution per hour. Some timers adapt easier than others, so you may want to shop around, and check out how others have done it. There are examples available on the Internet. Place the camera in the middle of the table for a family dinner and catch a time-lapse video of the event. Or place it in a room and use time-lapse to capture a 360 degree panorama.

Mountain Bike

Extreme mountain biking can include high speed runs, jumps, stunts, and plenty of air time and crashes. Mount your GoPro® camera to the handle bars and point it at the rider to create an action-shot selfie. Mount it on the side of the bike near the back, facing forward, for some interesting action shots during an exciting ride. Be mindful of the terrain and don't use any kind of a pole mount if it creates a risk that the camera will get hung up in brush or collide with a tree.

Musical Instruments

Many musical instruments can be used to create an interesting camera angle. It is not limited to just the guitar, drums, and keyboard. If you play in a marching band or a school orchestra, consider mounting several GoPro® cameras on instruments at an upcoming performance and then editing the video to show the performance from a whole new perspective.

Paintball

Mount a GoPro® camera on your paintball guns before your next match. Use the waterproof housing to protect the camera from flying paint.

Consider a few more cameras mounted to player's helmets or goggles for a player's point of view. The results will be exciting.

Parachute Drop

This parachute drop doesn't involve jumping out of a plane. This one is just for the camera. Make a small parachute that will carry your GoPro® camera. Add some foam pipe insulation around your camera housing for extra crash protection. Now take your camera to a few high places and throw it off, letting it drift slowly to the ground on the parachute. Have a buddy in the landing zone to catch and/or retrieve your camera. Now find some more creative high places where you can drop your camera. Run the film backwards to give the impression that the camera is rising.

Parasailing

Parasailing is similar to hang gliding, except a parasail is used instead of a rigid wing. There will be fewer options for mounting the camera, and the best options may be on the helmet or the body of the parasail pilot.

Parkour

The aim of Parkour is to run through an obstacle course and get from point A to point B in the most efficient way possible. Parkour typically involved lots of running, jumping, climbing, swinging, vaulting, rolling, and such. The GoPro® camera can be mounted at key obstacles to capture the view of the Parkour athletes as they pass, and it can also be mounted to the participant for point-of-view footage.

Pet Cam

Let your pet be the camera man! There are pet-friendly camera mounts that will hang the camera from a harness, or adapters can be built that add a camera mount to a pet's flotation life jacket. Whatever you do, make sure the camera will not put the animal at risk for getting hurt. Once the camera is in place, get some video of yourself playing with your dog, and splice in footage from both of your perspectives.

Playground

Children's playgrounds are filled with all kinds of exciting action and motion; monkey bars, climbing toys, slides, merry-go-rounds, and more. The GoPro® camera can be mounted easily to many of these play things for some great action shots. Let the kids have fun with it too. Mount a camera on a bike helmet and let kids take turns wearing it as they play. Teach some children how to use a monopod to take video of themselves as they run and play.

Put It in a Model Rocket

It will require a large model rocket, but it can be done! Modify the rocket so the GoPro® camera is looking out through an opening in the side of the rocket. Test the parachute to make sure it is adequate for the added weight. Start the camera rolling and fire it up into the sky.

Put It in a Nerf Football

Slice open a Nerf football with a sharp knife and carve out a cavity to hold the GoPro® camera. Position the camera so it is pointing out one end of the football. Set the camera far enough back from the end of the football so that there is some foam to protect the lens from damage during impact. Start the camera recording and then use duct tape to seal up the football. Now use the ball to throw a few perfect spiral passes. Experiment with the camera facing forward and facing to the rear as you throw.

Put it in the Dishwasher

This will require the use of a waterproof enclosure and a waterproof flashlight. Mount the camera in the dishwasher. Put the light in the dishwasher and turn on the light and the camera. Turn off the drying element so none of the plastic parts are exposed to high heat. Run the dishwasher for a little bit and you will have some interesting pictures of something we always hear, but never get to see.

QA an Umpire for Calling Balls and Strikes

Place a GoPro® camera on the catcher's mask during a baseball game. Video replay can't be used to call balls and strikes, but it can make for some interesting conversations after the game!

Quad Copter

Radio controlled quad copters are available with GoPro® camera mounts already built in. At the time of this writing there are several copters available for around $500 that include a camera mount and GPS navigation. The flight controls have been goof-proofed to make flying simple, even for beginners. Models with GPS will return to you and land with just the push of a single button. Be careful where you take pictures with a quad copter. Many areas are very skeptical of "drones" and in some cases there are local ordinances prohibiting their use for photography. People are worried they will be used to spy on people or take pictures of sensitive government installations.

RC Model Boat

Mount your camera to a radio controlled model boat for some unique picture taking opportunities. You can photograph a boat race, or use the craft to sneak up on wildlife. Use your waterproof enclosure for this. The added weight may slow a racing boat down a bit, so racers may not want to have this onboard during a race. But another boat out there with them can get some great shots that would not be possible with a manned camera.

RC Model Car

RC model cars are used in two major venues. Some are flat track racers that zip around race tracks built in vacant parking lots. Others are off road buggies that do lots of exciting jumps and flips to get over and around obstacles. Both types of driving can make some exciting video. You can do some things with a model car that you would not dare do if you were driving a real car. Use your GoPro® camera to catch all the action.

RC Plane

Place your GoPro® camera in a radio controlled model airplane for some great aerial photography. The camera is light enough to be carried easily by most modern model planes. The camera can face down, to the front, out one side, or looking back. Mount the camera in a location that does not change the balance of the aircraft, as this will have an impact on how it flies. It seems that if a camera is attached to a model airplane, modern society now calls it a "drone" and doesn't want it flying around their neighborhood. So be careful where you choose to take your aerial pictures so that no one feels like their privacy is being invaded.

Refrigerator Cam

Hide a GoPro® camera in your refrigerator the next time you have a party. Invite your guests to make themselves at home and help themselves to the cool beverages in the refrigerator. Use the footage later to add some interest to the other footage you took at the party.

Robotics Competition

Robotics competitions are a lot of fun. Kids build fabulous robotic contraptions and compete against each other to see which robot can best perform the challenge. The challenges vary, but usually include a lot of action. They might be picking up balls, throwing and retrieving Frisbees®, or solving some kind of a puzzle. Competitors may not want the camera on their robot during the competition because of the added weight, but they may not mind using one during practice. The onboard camera will give some fun filled footage of the event and will be nice when blended in with video taken from other angles.

Rock Climbing

Here is an extreme sport that can get you some great action shots. The camera will have to be mounted on a helmet or on a body strap. Additional cameras can be placed along the climbing route to catch the action as people climb on by. You might even work out a system in which the leader plants a few cameras on the way up, and the last person to pass by collects them. Always think safety first and avoid mounting cameras anywhere on a climber that can cause them to get hung up or tangled in gear.

Roller Skating

Think of all the creative ways you can use a GoPro® camera while roller skating. This may be one of the few times when it is acceptable to mount a camera on your shoes. You could also set the camera on the floor and skate around it, use a monopod to take some selfies, or mount it on your hat. A rear facing camera can be used to capture video of the people skating behind the camera operator.

Roomba Cam

Do you have a Roomba® robotic vacuum cleaner? Ever wonder where it goes and what it does when you are not home? Set up your GoPro®

camera on the back of your Roomba and turn it loose. This can be especially entertaining if you have a dog or a cat that likes to interact with the Roomba® while it is working.

Rope Swing

Imagine a rope swing hanging over your favorite swimming hole. Now think of all the ways you can use a GoPro® camera to capture the action as you and your friends swing out on the rope and drop into the water. Place a camera on the rope that looks down at the person as they swing. Place another camera on the very end of the rope to catch an unobstructed view of the jump and the splash. Let the jumper carry a camera on a monopod to capture the freefall and the dive into the water.

Sailing

Sailboats usually have lots of handrails and rigging that make good mounting spots for a GoPro® camera. You will find fun angles for watching the crew at work, watching the waves rush by, catching the motion of the sails, and perhaps even getting video of other nearby boats. Things get exciting when the big boats are racing, especially when starting a race or rounding a marker in a crowd. You will want to use a waterproof enclosure to protect the camera for this event.

Scavenger Hunt

Use GoPro® cameras on monopods to conduct a video scavenger hunt. Divide your group into teams and give them a list of activities to choose from. They must film their entire team participating in an activity on the list in order to score points for that activity. Set some ground rules first, such as no driving over the speed limit, and whatever other rules are appropriate for maintaining safety. Try to put enough things on the list so that it is not possible to do them all in the time limit. This will cause each team to have a unique collection of videos. Have everyone get back together at the designated time and enjoy a pizza feast while you have fun watching everyone's videos.

Scuba Dive

The waterproof dive housing of the GoPro® camera will keep the camera dry down to 197 feet (60 meters). You have to be very careful that there is no dirt, hair, or any debris on the white rubber seal when you close the housing. Any kind of lint on the seal can cause the housing to leak when it goes underwater. If you are using the camera in salt water, do a dunk test in fresh water first to check for leaks. If salt water leaks into the housing it can destroy the camera. There are dive masks with GoPro® camera mounts built in. You may also have good results by mounting a camera on the dive tanks or on the spear gun.

Sewer Pipe Inspection

So you think that underground pipe might have an obstruction? You might be able to see it with your GoPro® camera. If you can get a good angle on the opening of the pipe, you can insert a wand with your GoPro® camera and a small flashlight taped on the end. If the pipe is large enough, you can push the camera in far enough to see around a bend and view things you can't see just by looking in. You will definitely want the waterproof housing for this application. Wash everything off when you are done!

Side View Cam (Car)

The inspiration for this idea comes from those drivers who seem to always be using their cell phone while driving. Mount your GoPro® camera so that it is looking out the passenger side window and let it record for a while as you drive through town on multilane roads. If you happen to notice someone driving while texting, ride beside them for a few seconds to capture the video proof. With a good camera angle you might also get a look at the license plate as they pull away from you.

Skateboarding

Skateboarding is definitely a high energy action packed sport with lots of thrills, spills, and excitement. Cameras can be mounted on structures in a skate park, on the skateboard, and on the rider. Have you ever seen high definition video taken from underneath a skateboard? You can do that with a GoPro® camera. Just be very careful to ensure that there is enough clearance to prevent the camera from getting crushed, and avoid doing stunts that would cause the camera to impact a hard surface.

Sky Diving/Base Jumping

This is a very popular application for the GoPro® camera. Sky divers use GoPro® cameras on their helmets and on their extremities to capture footage of themselves and of their fellow jumpers. Some of the most frequently captured scenes include watching the jump plane fly away after the initial leap.

Snowmobiling

There are many different ways to enjoy a snowmobile ride. It might be a practical hunting trip, or a gentle trail ride. Or it might be an adrenaline filled day of hill climbing, jumping, and running away from avalanches. The GoPro® camera can be used to capture video or still images of these events without having to think about taking pictures. Mount one or more GoPro® cameras in waterproof housings on your snowmobile and start them recording at the beginning of your ride. Attach a bright colored ribbon to the camera to make it easier to find if it falls off in the snow. Avoid mounting the camera anywhere that will cause it to get covered with snow that is kicked up from the tracks. If snow is falling, remember to occasionally clean the camera housing to keep the snow off the lens. Edit the video later into a great memory of the day.

Speed Boat

Use your GoPro® camera to capture the action from lots of fun angles while speeding along in a power boat. Put the camera in a waterproof enclosure and attach it a monopod to film the waterline as the boat is on a plane. Place the camera on the dashboard to film the facial expressions of the captain and the crew. The waterproof enclosure will also protect the microphone from the wind noise.

Spin Children Around

This one is for strong adults who can play carefully with young children who like to be spun around. Mount the GoPro® camera to your helmet or to the front of your body. Now hold both of the wrists of your small friend and spin around gently, lifting their feet off the ground. The camera should be positioned to capture the smiles and the background as is zips around. Stop before you get too dizzy.

Stunt Kite

If you know how to fly a two line stunt kite, this can be a simple and affordable way to get your GoPro® camera up in the air while also having some control over where it is pointed. It will work best if the camera is mounted near the center of the kite so that it does not change the balance of the kite during flight. Kites with a rigid frame are usually easier to mount the camera on. It is also possible to make a camera mount using super strong neodymium magnets. The magnets can be used to attach the camera to the fabric of the kite. Use the Wi-Fi feature of the camera to get an idea of what the camera sees when the kite is airborne.

Surfing

Surfing was the inspiration that lead to the invention of the GoPro® camera, and is one of the reasons why most GoPro® camera outfits come with a waterproof enclosure. The camera can be mounted to the front or to the back of the board, held on a monopod, or be worn by the surfer. You can purchase floating monopods that will keep your camera on the surface if it is dropped.

Swing Set

Swinging on a swing set can create some interesting video footage when using a GoPro® camera. The camera can be mounted to the swing set chain, it can be worn by the person in the swing (such as on a shoe, looking up at the face), or it can be worn by someone pushing the swinger. Editing these various angles together can make a fun day on a swing set into a fond memory.

Tell Your Kids to Go Make a Movie

What do you do with a bunch of kids who are looking for something to do on a rainy day? Why not give them a GoPro® camera and tell them to go make a movie? They will be busy for hours working out their storyline, shooting the scenes, and then editing the final presentation. End the day with some good food and a family gathering to watch the movie.

Throw It

This activity will require a little preparation and some careful aiming. Place the camera in the waterproof enclosure for protection. Tape a few pieces of foam pipe insulation around the edges of the case to provide some cushion in case the camera is dropped. Once the camera is protected, toss it gently into the air and catch it. You are not likely to get a lot of video that you can use, but you will get a few seconds of very interesting motion that can become an interesting part of a larger project.

Tie It on a Long Pole or a Stick

The monopod is usually a relatively short handle, sometimes no more than a foot long. Some of them will extend to several feet. This idea takes the monopod to the extreme: mount the camera on a long pole and you can extend your reach to get shots that are otherwise impossible. Reach out across a stream to record video of a fishing hole or capture action on the river as rafters go by. Hold the camera up high and walk around your yard to simulate the effect of flying around your house. Once you get this set up and working you are bound to discover many uses for it.

Time-Lapse a Craft Project

Time-lapse photography is a fun way to add interest to any hobby or craft activity. It might be carving jack-o-lanterns, building a model, or creating a painting. Set up the GoPro® camera in time-lapse mode and speed up time for the replay and watch your project come together in high speed motion.

Time-Lapse a Home Improvement Project

This is like your craft project, but on a much larger scale. Are you painting a house? Mowing the lawn? Putting on a new roof? Mount your GoPro® camera on a tripod and film the action in time-lapse mode.

Time-Lapse of Nature

Nature provides us with many fun moving scenes that can be make interesting subjects for time-lapse photography. The GoPro® camera can capture images over a single day, or with a little work – over a season, or even an entire year. The possibilities are nearly without limit. A simple project to start with may be to simply film the clouds as they roll by slowly overhead. Or film the rise and fall of the tide.

Time-Lapse Vacation Cam

How can you show a full week of vacation video in just five minutes? With time-lapse photography! Set up the camera in time-lapse mode and point it at the action all week during your vacation. Point it out the front window of the car when traveling, or at the passengers in the back seat. Add your favorite song from the trip as your background music and edit the final results for a fun memory maker.

Trampoline

Use your GoPro® camera with a monopod to get exciting video of yourself jumping on the trampoline. Then position the camera for some unique shots from the edge of the trampoline and even underneath. If you are brave enough to jump together with a friend, use your camera to get some shots up close to the action.

Underwater Treasure Hunting

Have you ever seen how treasure hunters use a submarine to look for treasure on the bottom of the sea? You can do the same thing with your GoPro® camera and a weighted line. Place your camera in the waterproof housing and attach it to a weighted line. Get in a rowboat and start recording video of the underwater landscape by pulling the camera around the bay with the rowboat. Keep a log book of where you are at specific times during your treasure hunt. You can use the log notes later to estimate your location when viewing the video, just in case you find a treasure you need to return to.

Video Blog from Anywhere

The GoPro® camera is the perfect tool for a video blog. It is small enough to take anywhere, and it records high definition video that is higher in quality than most cell phone cameras. Using a monopod makes it easy to aim the camera at yourself, and the wide angle view makes it easy to capture the recording environment at the same time.

Water Ski

Place the GoPro® camera in the waterproof housing and mount it on the tow line just ahead of the handle. The camera will be able to record some underwater footage and then be pulled up out of the water to get a great close up of the water skier. There are some good action shots to be had through creative camera placement on the skis, on the skier, and on the boat. Cover multiple angles and mix them together for a fun action movie.

Water Slide

Never before has there been a camera better suited for a trip down a water slide than the GoPro® camera. Just make sure the water park doesn't have any rules against holding a camera while you go down the slide.

Weight Lifting

The lightweight GoPro® camera can get up close to those flexing muscles and capture some of those interesting facial expressions made during a workout or a competition. You can also mount the camera in a stationary position to film yourself and review the video later to see if you are using proper form as you lift.

Whitewater Rafting

Place the GoPro® camera in the waterproof housing and add some bright colored floatation to the case. Now mount one or more of these on the raft to capture the action. The wide angle setting will let you see the excitement in the river and the activity in the boat.

Windsurfing

Windsurfing is much more exciting to watch when you are on board! The GoPro® camera can be mounted on the back of the boom, or near the mast, or high on the mast looking down. Interesting camera angles can be achieved from the tail end of the board, and also from the front. Use the waterproof housing and add some bright colored floatation (just in case the camera gets away). Go land a few jumps and then show your land loving friends how exciting it really is when you are out there in the wind.

Zip Line

The obvious zip line is the one you get to ride on. Mounting a GoPro® camera to yourself is a great way to get pictures of your near-flight experience. But how about making a special zip line just for the camera? Bend some wire to make a camera mount that can slide down a piece of fishing line. Use a fishing pole to make your zip line. Stretch the line out through some interesting scenery and send your camera flying down the line. Now start thinking of all the places you can go to set up your instant zip line and get some interesting and unique near-flight video with your GoPro® camera.

ABOUT THE AUTHOR

Jim R. Larsen is a Technical Writer, Illustrator, and Instructional Designer. In his "day job" Jim creates online training and manages web development for a large state agency. In his spare time Jim has authored a successful series of books that instruct readers with practical knowledge on how to use simple engineering and technology to create fun projects.

Titles authored by Jim R. Larsen:

Quick and Easy Stirling Engine

Three LTD Stirling Engines You Can Build Without A Machine Shop

11 Stirling Engine Projects You Can Build

Jim R. Larsen books are available on all Amazon websites, at online bookstores, and by special order in any bookstore.

www.ingramcontent.com/pod-product-compliance
Lightning Source LLC
Chambersburg PA
CBHW070718180526
45167CB00004B/1528